Yoga Bees Are Beautiful

YOGA BEES ARE BEAUTIFUL
A Yoga Bee Press / BookBaby Book
September 2021

Designed by Tahji LaComb-Wolpert
Produced by abbydigital.com
Published by BookBaby in Pennsauken, NJ

ISBN: 978-1-09839-249-9

YOGA BEES ARE
BEAUTIFUL

By Tahji LaComb-Wolpert

Foreword by Rima Rabbath

YOGA BEE PRESS
New York, NY

BOOKBABY
Pennsauken, NJ

The Soul is the Bee

The Teacher is the Queen Bee

The Beehive is the Community (Sangat)

The Seat of Meditation is the Flower

The Buzz is the Eternal Om (Sound Current)

The Sun is the Light of Divinity

The Honey is the Yoga

Om Shanti Shanti Shanti

SATAJI

DEDICATED TO THE ALMIGHTY FOUNTAIN OF LOVE
WORKING THROUGH ALL MASTERS OF ALL TIMES
AND TO

PROFESSOR SATAJI YOGI

My deepest gratitude to Him for graciously bestowing upon me
the sweet nectar of the Holy Naam - the Word - the Eternal Om
and initiating me into the Divine path of Surat Shabd Yoga.
I feel your glorious presence and internal guidance
with me everywhere and at all times.

"When there is Honey, the Honeybees will come"

- SATAJI

In Dedication
and Service to
Sri Dharma Mittra,
Yoga Honeybee Supreme!

Disciple of Swami Kailashananda, Master of yoga, founder of Dharma Yoga Center NYC, teacher of teachers, beloved to the world - Extraordinaire!

This book is inspired by him and there is no way it would have manifested without him so patiently teaching us the way.

In Dedication
and Gratitude to
Rima Rabbath,
Queen Yoga Honeybee of Beauty,
Inspiration and Light!

Senior Jivamukti teacher,
creator of Souk,
friend to everyone.

A loyal student of Sharon Gannon, David Life and Pema Chödrön, Rima shares the way and dedicates her life to the Yoga Beehive.

A treasure house of kindness, compassion, understanding, truth and love.

CONTENTS

YOGA BEES ARE BEAUTIFUL
Foreword by Rima Rabbath

This book is fresh. "Fresh" as in new – new in the way the story of yoga is being told. Yoga is old, as old as a mountain - like Mount Kailash where Lord Shiva resides. When Shiva is not on the mountain meditating, he can be found by the river Ganga. Rivers too are very old. Mountains and rivers are ancient like the teachings of yoga. But the mountains and rivers are also here, now. We climb mountains and from their peak (if we get high enough), we can see more properly; our worldview expands. We sit by the bank of a river so that we can watch its flow and unstoppable energy, like the unstoppable energy of life, things endlessly arising and dissolving.

There is something so "refreshing" about this book. There is zero pretension to it. It's humble like its author, Tahji. She speaks of "Google time" in the most simple, hilarious way. If any aspect of the book captures our interest, she invites us to do some research on our own. Not only by reading ancient texts on yoga but also because so much information nowadays is shared on the world wide web – this vast network that connects us – why not look there too!

There is a dedication section early on in the book, a homage to all those who have inspired Tahji and taught her yoga. As I read it, I was reminded of the Hatha Yoga Pradipika, a manual on the practices of yoga. In that text, the author, Master Swatmarama, thanks every person who has helped him gain the knowledge of yoga, all the way back to Shiva. He even gives thanks to those he doesn't know by name as well as to those he has forgotten or overlooked. This is a poignant teaching because without acknowledgment of lineage, no meaningful transmission can happen. It is only when we can recognize those who have shared their knowledge with us that we are able to connect to the source. Only then, can we become a conduit, a channel, through which that knowledge can flow (like a river).

There is also a playful, enthusiastic, almost innocent quality to this book. Just the imagery of the bees buzzing around is invigorating. There is also a sense of urgency that we are nudged to cultivate now, which is what the very first quote in the book points to: **atha yoga anuśāsanam**.

Atha traditionally implies an auspicious beginning. It is a sacred word. So sacred that it ranks only second to Om. Atha calls our attention to the fact that something of great importance is about to happen now. Atha sets a certain mood, and that mood makes you want to enter the space following atha. Opening the book with this quote makes us feel invited to enter the world of yoga bees so that we can have a direct experience, a taste, of "the honey."

As I glossed over the book's pages at first and then dove more deeply, I was struck by how gently and subtly, in a most nuanced calligraphic and artistic way, we find ourselves becoming part of a community. We somehow become friends with the practitioners whose photos are part of this project but also with every teacher and master whose name is invoked in this book. We might be alone going through the book yet there is nothing lonely about the experience.

Finally, this heart-project says something about the possibilities that arise when we "move" as a community. The power of satsang or the sangha (which are Sanskrit words for community and association) is that one almost immediately feels in good company. The asanas portrayed in this book are not static. Instead, there is a dynamic quality to them that mirrors what a community is about. When we are part of a community, we act as mirror reflections, providing each other a continual reference point, which in turn creates a continual learning process.

Community becomes a source of learning that humbles us and softens us. We practice together, we encourage each other but we are also honest with one another. As Chögyam Trungpa Rinpoche, a Tibetan Buddhist teacher, writes: "The companionship within the sangha is a kind of clean friendship – without expectation, without demand, but at the same time, fulfilling."

To me, this book is an invitation to never stop making friends, with ourselves and with others. This is the source of true strength. **Maitrī** is the Sanskrit word for friendship. It also means friendliness, close contact, a feeling of approval or support. As my teacher, the co-founder of

Jivamukti Yoga, Sharon Gannon reminds us: "Through friendliness, kindness and compassion (**maitrī**), strength comes." (Commentary on Verse 24, Chapter 3 of The Yoga Sutras.)

This book will give you strength as it is offered with the friendliest and most welcoming intention - an intention that will pique your curiosity and encourage your participation in yoga.

I am so honored to have been asked to be part of this sweet beehive.

Thank you.

Rima Rabbath

INTRODUCTION

Welcome, Everyone! And I mean Everyone! Like yoga, this book is for everyone, and anyone can benefit from this book somehow and in some way. For example, you can read the book in its entirety or you can just browse the pictures. You can read just the dedications or the bibliography and find something interesting. You can decorate your table with it, give it as a gift, journal your thoughts about it or meditate on its very essence. The possibilities are endless. Wherever you are is perfect. I'm happy you have this book because I want to share with you the beauty of life from a yoga practitioner's perspective which can hopefully help and inspire you on your own personal life's path. Using this book is our yoga practice at this moment. It's a part of practice that's called self-study (swadhyaya niyama). Hopefully this book will shed some light onto your life and let you experience the joy and beauty lurking within yourself.

Let's start by making an intention for practicing with the book. My intention is that the book is charged with blessings, knowledge, love, beauty and joy, that it opens the space for everyone to be happy, and that happiness pours out into the world. It's a collective collage designed to lift the soul, inspire the heart and help one come into their ultimate self. This book is designed to work hand-in-hand with every other reference source you have in your life. In particular, your own life experiences and Google. Yes, Google! In this day and age and for the purpose of this book, we won't need to explain every word and concept or lay out the entire history of everything or overtalk. Whatever catches your soul strings, take the ball and run with it. Look up the words, research the quotes, cross reference it with your other books, or take it further by journaling your ideas and experiences, and perhaps sharing those with others. Feel free to reach out to me with any questions or insights you have along the way. Let it become a part of you. Relate it to your own life, in any way intuition guides you at the moment, and enjoy your experience. May the grace of intuition, creativity and oneness be with us all.

Another way we can make this a yogic experience/practice, whether or not you've ever been to a yoga class, is by applying the grand yoga rule numero uno while reading this book. Rule numero uno comes from a practice called Ahimsa, which means no harming, no violence, no killing. Yogis apply this practice in thought, word and deed to everything they do. I really want to mention this so that nobody bashes the book or harms anyone with it. Just kidding, but it would be nice if we could just enjoy the book without getting caught up in the judgmental mind which wants to criticize, condemn or get into some kind of negative reaction. If you see that is happening, and it is very common, just pause, take 1 to 3 deep breaths, reset an intention for practice, and start again. The beautiful thing about the mind is that we can have a new beginning whenever we want one. No need to wait for January 1st. And again, as we mentioned earlier, use it as self-study. Use it to get closer to the real you, the best you, the perfect, divine incarnation of love that you are.

The most famous of yoga questions is "Who am I?" It's probably also the most famously asked question of human beings (besides "what's for dinner?"). If this book becomes part of the quest to answer that question for you, that is yoga practice. Lastly, we can make this a yogic practice by offering all outcomes of this book to the Highest, and that can be whatever you can imagine the Highest to be. We can make it an offering from our hearts, and however we participate, it is in some way a practice of devotion. This practice comes from the teachings found in a spiritual roadmap book called The Bhagavad Gita (Google time BG ch2, v47 and ch9, v26). Enjoy being with this book, let go of all worry and stress, and let the simple joy of beauty unfold. Feel free to share any insight, ask any question or simply say hello at *tahji@ yogabeesarebeautiful.com*.

In Yoga Bees are Beautiful, we are going to find the sameness of the yoga practitioner and the honeybee. We are going to use the sweet remembrance of the honeybees' natural gifts to inspire and remind us that we too can use the same qualities to hie on our own unique paths. This book was first and foremost inspired by the beloved Sri Dharma Mittra. He is the bee, the flower, the honey and the sunshine all in one beautiful being. When I took his 200 hour yoga teacher training course in 1999/2000 he taught the course single-handedly and straight from his heart. He is the creator of one of the most famous yoga posters in the world called the "Master Chart of 908 Postures." I recommend you pause right here, find the chart on the internet and take a peek! Taking an expression from my Jivamukti Yoga teacher Rima, this chart is "Amaze-Balls!" If you can't see the chart, imagine a 43"x 60" sized poster with a large Om symbol in the middle overlayed with rows and rows of different yoga asanas (poses). This chart was created and executed by Sri Dharma himself. When he taught this teacher training program, he taught the entire chart. He went from the very first pose, #1 of the Sun Salutation, called the Mountain Pose, (the sun salutation is a sequence of poses strung together and practiced as a meditative flow of movement) all the way to the last pose Nauli, a breathing pose which was pose #908. He taught us how to do the entire treasure trove of poses in between #1 and #908, and how to teach them.

When I took his teacher training course, I was a professional dancer and was up for trying each and every pose. Dharma always had the gift of teaching telepathically and he could get your body into a pose bypassing the thinking mind and taking you into a deeper state of consciousness. One day he had me demonstrate backbends from the chart. We started at wheel asana preparation #519, lifted up the heart, chest and front body to a backbend pushing with the hands and feet, and proceeded through to #534 which was a really extreme version of this pose with one leg extended towards the ceiling. Then, through transmission and minimal instruction, he told me to place both feet on the floor and to hold each foot with my hands one at a time. I miraculously did #536. He said to the class, "See how that makes a full wheel? It's a complete circle." It was easy and effortless at that moment and probably one of the hardest balances I've ever done. That was the one and only time I ever could do that pose. Let me just note, there is a #537 and Dharma is the only person I've ever seen do it this well. #537 is called Vertical Leg Split Pose. You're in #536, hold one foot with both hands and extend the free leg perfectly vertically into the air! Voila!

Besides teaching us every pose in the chart, which was beyond fun and inspiring, he started plugging into our heads the notion that we could all make our own posters. He never did assign this project, but the way he mentioned it, I started planning to make my own chart, in case he made it a requirement to pass the course. He didn't, but the seed was planted.

Sataji, my spiritual teacher since 1993, with whom I have studied to whom I have been devoted to ever since, left me a legacy of a yoga studio called the Yoga Den. Professor Sataji Yogi was a teacher of Surat Shabd Yoga (Light and Sound meditation). He taught the Path of the Masters through the guidance and instruction of his beloved guru. This form of yoga was focused on meditation and ethical conduct. It was founded upon the similar practices amongst all spiritual masters which all lead to the same spiritual Truths. Sataji himself did not teach postures but believed doing yoga postures was conducive to a healthier body and a quieter mind. He thought offering yoga classes that taught postures would be a good preparation for the type of meditation he taught and would be of service to the community. He's the one who sent me to Sri Dharma to be certified to teach yoga. The Yoga Den has been a lifeline for me in every imaginable way. My entire life and human revolution revolve around this most wonderful gift.

In 2003, as the Yoga Den was progressing, I wanted to do something that would challenge some of my younger students to practice the yoga teachings in the world outside the yoga studio. I also wanted to make an offering of some type to Sataji, my teachers, friends, family and community. At this time, we had an amazing group of teenage students, many of whom also studied at the world-renowned School of American Ballet in New York City. Can you still make it in the world and really stick to the yogic teachings such as non-harming, truthfulness, and non-greed at the same time? The answer is: yes you can, but it takes overcoming obstacles and refining your experiences to master it. Finally, the inspiration came to make a Yoga Den calendar with pictures of them with yogic quotes under their pictures. This process would bring out the inner challenges one could predict, similar to those they may face in the dance world. When they got jealous, frustrated, angry, greedy, egotistical, etc., the opportunities to put the teachings to work manifested. This in turn helped them stay grounded, focused, happy, calm and together! It worked out as hoped.

One girl, Triang, who was a little shy would be the calendar designer. My professional dance photographer, Eduardo Patino, would do the photography. The photos could also be used as a steppingstone towards creating a poster one day. We created calendars for 2003, 2004 and 2006. The photography was beautiful, and the process turned us all into yoga honeybees buzzing all around, buzz, buzz, buzz. We were immersed in the teachings like the bee immersed in the flowers. We were gathering the nectar through Divinity's Grace. The honey was being produced from the process. We practiced the 8 limbs of classical hatha raja yoga all the way through, focusing intently on the Yamas (restraints) and Niyamas (observances). Sri Dharma says there's no yoga without the Yamas and Niyamas and he's right! Surprise, surprise!

Bees symbolize community and unity. Community is often experienced when you start practicing yoga. Yoga itself means "union," technically "to yolk together." It is the science of connection. This community and unity through connection happens on all levels. These levels are physical, mental, psychic and spiritual. We try to discover and unfold the oneness of all that exists within ourselves, our community and the world. The highest aim and goal of practicing yoga is Self-Realization. The bees build their community gradually. They start small and build up. They're hard working, they feed on the sweet nectar of flowers, they're non-harming and they serve, serve, serve. They produce honey which is delectably sweet, and they share with others.

Likewise, this is how a yoga community builds. The soul (individual) is the bee. The teacher is the queen bee. The community is the beehive. The seat of meditation is the flower. The buzz of the bee that resounds within and without is the Shabd, the Word, the Om or the Eternal Sound of creation. The Self-Realization, the yogic experience and the peace, love and joy that unfold from all of this is the sweet, golden honey. The flowers symbolize anyone or anything that feeds us inspiration and physical, mental, and/or spiritual nourishment. The flower also symbolizes beauty, truth and the spiritual fragrance of a yogi. When we say the flower is the seat of meditation, it means we are grounded in these traits. The flower also symbolizes that which we are physically balancing on when we are practicing yoga such as a mat, cushion, a chair or the Earth itself. The bee also symbolizes focus. In yoga we want to control our attention and perfect our focus. We want single-pointed attention like the bee. To get there we practice a personalized combination of techniques. Meditation and mindfulness are two of those techniques. Activity, discipline, diligence and living in ways that cause the least amount of harm are also the things the bees and yogis have in common. The sunshine symbolizes the Supreme Divinity.

The Yoga Den, like any school of yoga, is symbolic of a beehive in nature, and everyone who comes in and out of it becomes a yoga bee of some sort. When we ingest that which is sweet what comes out is only bound to be sweet as well. I would like to take this moment to introduce the yoga bees that grace the many pages of the photographs in this book. Abby Simon was the first of these bees to start attending classes at the Yoga Den. She was unique in that she was young, and she was an aspiring ballerina. She soon started bringing her family and her friends and then her friends started bringing their family and friends. Of these, you will see sisters Cassia and Zoey, sisters Ariel and Adrian, brother and sister Tanner and Courtney, and friends Abigail, Miriam, Emily, Marika and Giovanni. You will also see me, Lucy, James and their daughter Zoë. These photos of the yoga bees were all shot by Eduardo Patino and I'm very excited for you to see them. Eduardo is an amazing, intuitive and dynamic photographer and knows how to capture the exhilarating beauty of what he is shooting. The credits page in the back will list for you who's who and the pages on which each person appears.

The illustrations are by Giuliana Cassataro, another bee from the Yoga Den beehive. She is a yoga teacher, yoga student, writer, artist and mother. She's basically a yoga bee deluxe. Each time you look at her work it brings out more of the simple joy and happiness that is within. The Om illustrations are intended as a special offering to Sri Dharma as he's the one who inspired them by having me draw Oms in every way imaginable. In the 500 hour teacher training course, which I completed during the 2020 global pandemic, Dharma went into great detail on guiding us how to draw and imagine Om. The Oms represent the eternal vibrations of Divinity that permeate everything. It's technically not a word, but a vibration. Lacing them throughout the book reminds us that everything is created and sustained by these vibrations. The more connected we stay with that, the more connected to everything we are in general.

Giuliana's mandala and symbol artwork help make space for us to go deeper within as we read the book with intuition, intention and stillness. Her color palette is exquisite and helps bring forth the vibrational absorption of the teachings in a simple, meditative way for everyone. The bees within the artwork remind us of the qualities of discipline, hard work, unity and love that go into the victory of achieving all that is challenging. Like these beautiful illustrations, each and every photograph in this book exemplifies those qualities.

My prayer is that this book becomes a source of joy and inspiration in your life. I pray it goes well with your furniture (just kidding). I hope in some way it is included in your journey of becoming the greatest you ever. I think this book can create another magnificent beehive amongst us. The sweet honey of joy and oneness can inspire new creations, interests and determinations from all of us. The yoga bee life is beautiful. Everything about yoga is Divine and blessed. Sataji always said yoga is for everyone. He said yoga is God's medicine. Many of us actually engage in activities that we never even realized were yogic practices. These would include helping others, telling the truth, self-study and making efforts to be kind. You might not be able to see yourself as a yoga bee quite yet, but that's what is so exciting about yoga. It's something you actually discover within yourself over time! For every practice, you start to realize that everything important is within you already. It's exciting and that excitement makes us start to work, focus and grow in a way that brings forth our own inner happiness.

It's important you always go at your own pace regardless of your level of experience and you don't push from the ego. Be true to your highest possible self and let your life unfold perfectly. Let everything be and watch it all come together in unison and perfection. We can keep the teachings very simple. We can take the lessons from the bees who remind us that non-harming, service, discipline, hard work and unity through community with the help of the All-Pervading Sunshine brings forth the honey. I hope this book is nectar and nourishment for you and helps you stay inspired, heal, spread your beauty everywhere and attain the Highest! In love and good intention, welcome to Yoga Bees are Beautiful. Deep breath in, slow breath out. Let's begin.

"ATHA YOGANUSASANAM"

- Patanjali Yoga Sutra 1.1

NOW IS THE TIME
FOR THE PRACTICE AND TEACHINGS OF YOGA

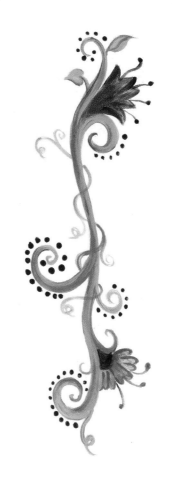

*"The aim and
The goal and
The purpose of yoga
Is to achieve
The state of oneness."*

- SATAJI

*"This above all: to thine own self be true and
Then it must follow, as night the day,
Thou canst not then be false to any man."*

- William Shakespeare

"You are part of an Infinite Energy...
Continuously remember it and feel it."

- OSHO

*"What people say
You cannot do,
You try and find out
That you can do."*

- HENRY DAVID THOREAU

*"Success comes
Where there is
Commitment."*

- SWAMI SIVANANDA

"Work is love made visible."

- KAHLIL GIBRAN

"Light the lamp of love and faith within you
And move forward."

- AMMA

*"So don't ever forget that
Any achievement in life
Is based on discipline."*

- SWAMI SATCHIDANANDA

"Perfection walks slow.
The time factor is necessary.
Go on, regularly;
After sometime you'll find
That you are on the way up."

- KIRPAL SINGH

"Be fearless, drop fears, be open."

- Osho

*"Behold! My heart dances to
The delight of a hundred arts,
And the Creator is
Well pleased."*

- KABIR

"Avail yourself of all Opportunities. Every Opportunity is meant for Your uplift and Development."

- SWAMI SIVANANDA

"Look within and behold your fortune."

- KABIR

"Know that every minute
That great presence is
In you, functioning
Through you, and you
Are nothing but an
Instrument."

- SWAMI SATCHIDANANDA

"Beauty is eternity gazing
At itself in a
Mirror."

- Kahlil Gibran

"Love has no other desire
But to fulfill itself."

- KAHLIL GIBRAN

"Let there be peace on earth
And let it begin with me."

- JILL JACKSON AND SY MILLER

"Flood the young brain
With healthy thoughts, ideas
And ideals."

- SWAMI SIVANANDA

"Be natural and you will Flower."

- OSHO

Breathe,
Relax everything,
Let go,
Be still.
Say to yourself
Who am I,
Who am I,
Who am I?"

- TAHJI/SATAJI

"Stay focused and
Joy will flow."

- KABIR

"There are many things
In life that will catch
Your eye, but only a few
That will catch your
Heart, pursue these."

- MICHAEL NOLAN

*"Whenever two persons meet,
A new world is created."*

- OSHO

*"Whenever one helps another,
Both are strong."*

- GERMAN PROVERB

*It is when you give of yourself that
You truly give."*

- KAHLIL GIBRAN

"Satyam Shivam Sundaram"
Truth, Godliness, Beauty

- INDIAN PHILOSOPHY

"Through activity energy
Is not lost -
Through activity
You renew it."

— OSHO

72

"It is through our efforts to
Achieve a flexible mind
That we can nurture
Resiliency of the human
Spirit."

- DALAI LAMA

*"Absorbed in life's beauty
I speak from the heart;
I listen from the heart."*

- KABIR

*"Your love is hiding within you.
Look there to succeed."*

- KABIR

"yad yad ācharati śhreṣhṭhas /
tad tad evetaro janaḥ
sa yat pramāṇaṁ kurute /
lokas tad anuvartate"

- BHAGAVAD GITA CHAPTER 3 VERSE 21

"A great person
Leads by example,
Setting standards that
Are followed by others
All over the
World."

- TRANSLATION: SHARON GANNON

"Endless love is
Raining down, it is
Always pouring joy."

- KABIR

*"A healthy
Sense of
Self-confidence
Is a
Critical factor
In
Achieving
Our goals."*

- DALAI LAMA

*"When you take each step with good thoughts
And a smiling face, all goodness will
Come and fill your being."*

- AMMA

"oṁ pūrṇam adaḥ pūrṇam idaṁ
pūrṇāt pūrṇam udacyate
pūrṇasya pūrṇam ādāya
pūrṇam evāvaśiṣyate"

- FROM YAJUR VEDA AND THE ISHA UPANISHADS

"That is whole. This is whole.
From the whole the whole
Becomes manifest. From the
Whole when the whole is
Negated, what remains again
Is the whole."

- TRANSLATION: SHARON GANNON

"Enjoy, celebrate,
Be active and
Always be a
Giver."

- OSHO

"Negatively judging others
Only darkens the landscapes
Within. Be still and
Be the beauty that
Lies within."

- TAHJI

"Meditate until every reproach
And hatred disappears, and
Compassion and love rise
Like a well of fresh water
Within you. Vow to work
For awareness and
Reconciliation by the
Most silent and
Unpretentious means
Possible."

- THICH NHAT HANH

*"When you are quiet,
You see everything
With love."*

- Sri Dharma Mittra

*"Thousands of candles can
Be lit from a single
Candle and the life of the
Candle will not be shortened.
Happiness never decreases from
Being shared."*

- BUDDHA

*"There is a divine purpose behind the
Life of everyone who comes into
The world. No one has been created
For nothing. We have something to
Learn from everyone. This is the
Secret of humility."*

- KIRPAL SINGH

"That which comes
From the heart
Will go to the
Heart."

- KIRPAL SINGH

*"The knower of the
Mystery of sound
Knows the mystery
Of the whole
Universe."*

- SUFI MYSTIC, HAZRAT INAYAT KHAN

"The soul unfolds itself
Like a lotus of
Countless petals."

- KAHLIL GIBRAN

"Know Thyself"

- ANCIENT GREEK APHORISM

111

"In the still mind the self reveals
Itself. From the depth of meditation, a
Person draws the joy and peace
Of complete fulfillment.

Having attained that abiding joy
Beyond the senses, revealed in the
Stilled mind, he will never swerve
From the eternal truth that
All life is one."

- BHAGAVAD GITA CHAPTER 6, VERSES 20-21

"So Ham"
I am That

- UPANISHADS

"Abiding joy comes to
those who still the mind."

- BHAGAVAD GITA CHAPTER 6, VERSE 27

"And there the
Bee of the heart
Is deeply immersed
And desires no
Other joy."

- KABIR

You are a Yoga Bee

You are Beautiful!

Joy

Joy

Joy

CONCLUSION

I hope that reading this book has been a fun and wonderful experience for you and that you have enjoyed it as much as my mom did. Just kidding, because that's impossible. FYI, my mom is a wonderful yoga bee who, at 80 years old, has just recently taken her yoga practice to a grand new level. Her whole life now is buzz, buzz, buzz. I read her the entire book over FaceTime, and she gave me the confidence needed to share it with you. The biggest challenge of this book was putting into words, illustrations and photos some things that are so simply and perfectly conveyed in the silence. I am urging everyone here to meditate. Wherever you are in your yoga bee journey, either start to meditate or, if you're a more experienced yoga bee, meditate, meditate, meditate. Concentrate. Be present. Bring forth your most incredible you and be happy. We see that in life the qualities to be successful in both the inner and outer worlds are the same. These are the qualities of our honeybees, which are discipline, focus, working together, serving, doing our best, feeding on what's sweet and beautiful, and doing as little harm along the way as possible. To be truly successful we need to summon these qualities deep from within ourselves and practice them with honesty, intention and love.

Sataji passed on to us the teaching that meditation is food for the soul. The soul communing with the Over-Soul is the purest, healthiest food the soul can feed on, and in nourishing yourself with it one becomes, with time, self-realized. The soul experiences its oneness with the Over-Soul and realizes the Over-Soul permeates everything. Therefore, the purest form of love, equality and Oneness is revealed within the Self. One with all and attaining self-knowledge, the highest knowledge attainable in the human form, one becomes a beacon of love, life and light like pure golden honey!

I'd like to entertain the practice of looking at this conclusion, or any conclusion for that matter, as a new beginning. The conclusion acts as a diving board springing us into a new place of creativity, spirituality, joy and stillness. A conscious conclusion has the power to ground us in a new, inspired place with gratitude and curiosity pulsing through ourselves like the sweetness of honey permeating our bloodstream. Let's be as one within as the bees in the beehive basking in the Divine Sunshine as we become conscious coworkers of the Divine Plan. The nourishing honey of love and Divinity can beautifully manifest for the benefit of all. Let's devote ourselves to being the best we can be for ourselves, others and our Creator. Yoga teaches us love and oneness. It teaches us to learn from everybody and everything. The practice of yoga, in any myriad of ways we practice it, can be what gets us to that point of joy and realization where we are completely immersed in happiness that desires nothing else and is always there.

There are so many ways to practice yoga and deepen our path towards ultimate fulfillment. Traditional yoga classes are an option, but not the only option. There's an unlimited number of ways we can participate whether we are intellectuals, artists, workers or all of the above. There are innumerable ways if we open our hearts and minds. Take it from wherever you are and call it to you. The right ways and the right teachers and the right support will come to you. Keep opening your mind to the possibilities. Ask around, Google around or personally reach out to me for suggestions. Keep things simple, keep it loving and remember, don't push. Trust yourself and remember you are part of the yoga bee community. Let's fly forward with smiles of gladness. Sant Kirpal Singh used to always say "Go Jolly!" He meant whatever you do and wherever you go, do it with a big lovingly jolly smile on the inside and the outside. Wishing everyone love from the deepest place possible in my soul and encouraging you all to come back again and again to this book to remember how much you are loved and needed. Take everything one step at a time. Try not to get caught up in comparing yourselves to others. The practice of not comparing ourselves to others is difficult, but very important. There's no freedom in comparing. Comparing is fear and is of a dualistic focus. We want single-pointed focus, absolute focus! Everything is One. Everything is equal. It's all Love. Your discipline, hard work and practice will always look different because you are unique and because you are special, not because something is wrong with you. Yoga is remembering that the unity and Oneness already exist! Don't compare. Bees don't compare. Let us soar on and live our lives with purpose and buzz. Let us drink the nectar, see the light and become pure honey. Joy and peace to everything and everybody.

Along with my mother's blessing, this book couldn't have come to us in this very special way without the blessings of Sataji, Sri Dharma and Rima. Sataji taught me to always look for the symbols in everything! He opened my eyes to the Eternal Sunshine and the True Buzz. Sri Dharma taught me that all the ideas are already out there, and that it's just a matter of using them. He taught me and is still teaching me yoga (I am now working towards the 800 hour certification). Rima taught me how to communicate to others by using simple examples from our lives. She gave me the space to "bee." She is forever an example of beauty, inspiration and being yourself.

I have tried to apply the truths of yoga I've been taught as I understand them at this moment, in making this book. I have joyfully tried to be honest with you and myself and hopefully everything is accredited properly. If it is not, please be a good yoga bee friend and let me know! Please!!! I would very much appreciate it and fix it for next time. I have tried to create this book according to inner instruction from within and have avoided trying to be competitive, self-assertive or deceptive in any way. I tried to work with intention and loving kindness. Hopefully I have been able to share with you the beauty of the yoga bee way of living and being. It really is an amazing way to live. A longer gratitude page awaits at the very end. There is a blank line on the gratitude page for you to put your name or initials on it. I am thankful you have offered your precious time and attention to reading this book! Please email me at tahji@yogabeesarebeautiful.com to share ideas or give feedback. I would love to hear from you. If you need a recommendation of where to find online yoga / meditation classes, you could start by looking at:

- www.dharmayogacenter.com
- www.soukofrima.com
- www.yogabeesarebeautiful.com

So, my dear, sweet, beloved yoga bees, let's conclude by chanting "Om Om Om / Lokah Samasta Sukhino Bhavantu / Om Shanti Shanti Shanti / Om Prem Gurudev" (Google time, but basically, let's feel the vibration of love everywhere / let's pray diligently for the freedom and happiness of all / Infinite Peace, Peace, Peace / All love to the Giver of Light within). Thank you for buzzing, keep on buzzing and may your moments all be nectar sweet and honey producing. Namaste Sweet Friends. Joy, Joy, Joy!

- Tahji

GRATITUDE & APPRECIATION

Special thanks and shout outs to the following and TO EACH AND EVERYONE OF YOU!

Sataji & Sat Nam Fellowship, Dharma Mittra & Dharma Yoga Center NYC
Rima Rabbath & Souk

Eduardo Patino, Giuliana Cassataro, Julia Valentine, Abby Digital, Dhira, Tira & Mira
Abby, Abigail, Adrian, Ariel, Cassia, Courtney, Emily, Giovanni, Marika, Miriam, Tanner, Zoey,
James, Lucy & Zoë
Mary & Linda Rodgers
My beloved husband Gregg who is the best there is,
Jeffrey, Natalie, grandchildren Annabelle, Serena, Luna & Gemma
My amazing mom Charlotte, Laurie & Paul, Jenny & Jeff, nieces & nephews Alex, Alejandra,
Mia, Kayla, Finn, and Miles
My superstar dad Bill and my stepmother Lorrie
The Yoga Den and the worldwide yoga community
Al Tischhauser, Katina Smalls and The Manhattan Athletic Club
To all my precious students everywhere
Evanston Township Highschool, SUNY@Purchase, School of American Ballet,
Martha Graham School, Joseph Pilates, George Mamales, Bert Terborgh, Kazuko Hirabyashi,
BKS Iyengar, Swami Sivananda, Govindas & Radha - Bhakti Yoga Shala, Jivamukti Yoga,
Krishna Das, Hagit Berdishevsky, Karen Perlia, Jamel Gaines & Creative Outlet,
Dave Lipshutz, Ceasar Puello, Dr. Ron Safko, Songki, Uncle & Bono, Michael Mao,
Chuck Golden, Leila, Mufasa, Jyoti, Ceasar & Orion.
To all Masters of Love, Light and Life everywhere and of all times.
And especially to you _____ (please put your name or initials!)

Gratitude, Salutations, Namastes and Love in abundance! THANK YOU!

Thank you so much to everyone!
Om Shanti
Guru Dev

Peace to you
Peace to all your loved ones
Peace to everything you touch
Peace to your enemies
Peace to this whole creation!

Namaste
&
Love

tahji

ABOUT THE ARTISTS

Eduardo Patino has been one of the leading Performing Arts Photographers over the past 20 years. He has built his reputation on an extraordinary understanding of the human figure, whether it is for portraiture, advertising or photographing the arts. Understanding athleticism, having been a former High School Quarterback turned dancer; his images communicate a strong sense of timing, line, movement, mood and lighting. His intrinsic knowledge for how the body moves allows him to capture the exact peak of movement or moment, whether for a full body view or a dynamic portrait.

www.epatinophoto.com

Tahji (Beth) LaComb-Wolpert has always loved photography, drawing, dance, yoga and life. She danced professionally for 15 years, traveling around the world, and has taught yoga and Pilates for over 25 years. Her credits include a BFA in dance & choreography from SUNY at Purchase, a 500 hour yoga teaching certification from Dharma Mittra, a 75 hour Spiritual Warrior certification from Jivamukti and an ordainment to instruct meditation practice from Professor Sataji Yogi. Her passion has always been unity and her art form has always been  what she calls "Collective Collage" which is the art of presenting a combination of elements to reveal an inherent mystic oneness. She hopes you love the book, and you remember to come back to it again and again so all its love, joy, inspiration and meaning will manifest in your life in a very simple, natural and fun way.

www.yogabeesarebeautiful.com

Giuliana Cassataro was born with a strong need for creativity and has always been drawn to the arts in all forms. She started drawing from the time she could hold a pencil and it has been a consistent form of creative expression ever since. She studied fashion and illustration at The Fashion Institute of Technology in NYC and has worked in the fashion industry. She was led to the Yoga Den in 1999 where she met Tahji and Sataji and fell in love with yoga. Under Sataji's loving guidance she went on to complete her yoga teacher training at the Sivananda Yoga Vedanta Center and her Yoga of the Heart training with Nischala Joy Devi. Yoga, meditation and the arts have been central to Giuliana's health, healing and happiness. She is currently working on different creative projects, including writing and illustrating children's books.

instagram.com/yamuna_creations_by_giuliana

CREDITS

ILLUSTRATIONS
Giuliana Cassataro

PHOTOS
Sataji, pg. vii - Miraji Gregory
Dharma Mittra (dark striped shirt), pg. ix - Gio Maldonado
(white shirt), pg. 81 - Jeffrey Vock
(Both photos courtesy of Yoga Dharma Center NYC)
Rima Rabbath, pg. ix - Peter Stanglmayr
Eduardo Patino, pg. 122 - Juan Patino
Giuliana Cassatro, pg. 122 - (courtesy of Yamuna Designs)
Tahji LaComb-Wolpert, pg. 122 - Christopher Saint Armand

EDUARDO PATINO PHOTOS
Marika Anderson, pgs. 33, 43, 45, 69, 71, 73, 91, 126, 127
Abigail Arzoumanov (Crutchfield), pgs. 15, 23, 35, 40, 41, 47, 66, 71, 73, 95
Cassia Burke, pgs. 44, 47, 56, 57, 59, 69, 91, 113
Emily Hayden-Rassel, pgs. 23, 24, 45, 47, 91
Tahji LaComb-Wolpert, pgs. 4, 17, 19, 37, 53, 67, 79, 89, 102, 103, 107, 121
Adrian Merrick, pgs. 23, 30, 37, 65, 71, 73, 75, 101, 105
Ariel Merrick, pgs. x, 23, 30, 31, 71, 73, 76, 77, 105
Zoey Phillips, pgs. xii, 21, 23, 27, 35, 37, 40, 41, 45, 47, 50, 51, 59, 60, 62, 63, 64, 65,
71 73, 82, 83, 92, 93, 98, 99, 105
Miriam Rowan, pgs. 47, 61, 69, 91, 96, 97
Courtney Schwartz, pgs. 47, 48, 49, 64
Tanner Schwartz, pgs. 18, 19, 39, 47, 55, 62, 64, 121
Abby Simon, pgs. ii, 13, 23, 25, 39, 47, 61, 63, 64, 65, 71, 73, 85, 86, 87, 91
James Veltri, pgs. 18, 19, 47, 121
Lucy Veltri, pgs. 28, 29, 47, 58
Zoë Veltri, pg. 58
Giovanni Villalobos, pgs. 18, 19, 23, 27, 35, 36, 40, 41, 44, 45, 47, 55, 59, 60, 65, 71, 73,
84, 98, 121

YOGA BEES ARE BEAUTIFUL ADVISERS
Gregg Wolpert, Dhira Bluestone, Julia Valentine, Charlotte LaComb,
Laurie LaComb and Giuliana Cassataro

BIBLIOGRAPHY

Amritananandamayi Devi, Sri Matta, Amma. July 1, 2000. *Light the Lamp of Love*
Amritapuri.org

Bluestone,Dhira, 1998. NYU News,
Yoga: The Key To Health and Happiness in Today's World [Video].

Buddha, Shakyamuni (retrieved 2021). *BrainyQuote.*
Brainyquote.com, (page unknown)

Easwaran, Eknath. *The End of Sorrow: The Bhagavad Gita Volume 1.*
Tomales, Nilgiri Press, April 2, 1993.

Ganon, Sharon. *JIVAMUKTI YOGA CHANT BOOK.*
New York, Sharon Ganon, 2003.

Gibran, Kahlil. *The Prophet.*
New York, Alfred A. Knoph, 1923.

Gyatso, Tenzin and Cutler, Howard. *The Art of Happiness.*
New York, Penguin Putnam Inc., 1998.

Hanh, Thich Nhat. *The Miracle of Mindfulness.*
Boston, Beacon Press, 1992

"Henry David Thoreau Quotes." Quotes.net.
STANDS4 LLC, 2021. Web.8 Feb. 2021.
https://www.quotes.net/quote/4847.

Kaupish, Kaylin (2021). www.guideposts.org.
The Spiritual Importance of Honeybees, page unknown

Khan, Hazrat Inayat (2021). www.goodreads.com
page unknown

Miller, Jill and Sy. *"Let There Be Peace on Earth".*
International Children's Choir, 1955.

Mittra, Sri Dharma. *Yoga Wisdom.*
New York, Dharma Yoga New York Center, 2017.

Mittra, Dharma (date unknown). www.quotemaster.com.
(Pintrest/FaceBook)

Nolan, Michael (2021). www.goodreads.com.
  page unknown

Osho. My Way: *The Way of the White Clouds*.
  Mumbai, Rebel Publishing house, 2009.

Osho. *When the Shoe Fits*.
  London, Watkins Publishing, 2006.

Osho, (2021). OSHOOnline
  Oshoonline.com (page unknown)

Rao, Sushil. *The Thirsty Fish* Kabir Kabir Bhajan.
  Forest Hills, Hrdaipress, 1997.

Satchidananda, Sri Swami. *The YOGA SUTRAS of PATANJALI*.
  Yogaville, Integral Yoga Publications, 1990.

Satchidananda, Swami (@Satciidananda).
  "So don't ever forget that any achievement in life is based on discipline."
  1/17/2016. Tweet.

Satchidananda Maharaj, Swami (2019).
  Sjnschool.com/testimonials/quote-15

Shakespeare, William. *Hamlet*.
  New York, Oxford University Press, 2009

Singh, Kirpal. *THE CROWN OF LIFE*.
  Delhi, Ruhani Satsang, 1961.

Singh, Kirpal. *Heart to Heart Talks Volume One*.
  Delhi, A.R. Manocha, Secretary, Ruhani Satsang, 1969-1970.

Singh, Kirpal. *The Way of the Saints*.
  Sanbornton, Sant Bani Ashram, 1976.

Sivananda, Sri Swami. *Thought Power*.
  Himalayas, The Divine Life Society, 1996.

Tagore, Rabindranath. *Songs of Kabir*.
  Boston, Red Wheel/Weiser, LLC, 2002.